WORLD ISSUES

NEW EUROPE

A look at the way the world is today

Antony Mason

Franklin Watts

ABOUT THIS BOOK

The expansion of the European Union in May 2004 created the world's largest trading bloc and the biggest single grouping of humanity on the planet after China and India. It also promised to heal the historic divide between eastern and western Europe that was forged during the communist era and the Cold War. This book explores how the enlargements of 2004 and 2007 have changed the character of the European Union and the challenges that lie ahead.

New updated edition printed in 2007
© Aladdin Books Ltd 2007
Produced by Aladdin Books Ltd
2/3 Fitzroy Mews, London W1T 6DF

ISBN 978–07496–7599–8 (Paperback)
ISBN 978–07496–7685–8 (Hardback)

Original edition first published in 2005 by

Franklin Watts	Franklin Watts Australia
338 Euston Road	Level 17/207 Kent Street
London NW1 3BH	Sydney NSW 2000

Franklin Watts is a division of Hachette Children's Books.

Designers: Flick, Book Design and Graphics
Pete Bennett – PBD
Editor: Katie Harker
Picture Research: Brian Hunter Smart

The author, Antony Mason, is a freelance editor and author of more than 60 books for both children and adults. He has written a number of books on 20th century history, and several guidebooks to Brussels and Belgium.

Printed in Malaysia   All rights reserved
A CIP catalogue record for this book is available from the British Library.
Dewey Classification: 341.242'2

CONTENTS

INTRODUCTION

The European Union (EU) was founded some fifty years ago to promote trade, peace and prosperity among its member nations. From the 1950s, the number of member states steadily grew from six to fifteen. Then in 2004, the EU increased its membership to 25 nations, and a further two countries joined in 2007.

The EU now spans three time zones stretching from the Baltic to the Mediterranean, and from the Atlantic Ocean to the Black Sea. Within its borders lie many of the world's most prosperous and vibrant countries. As a club of 27 nations, the EU has become a major force on the world stage, in trade, politics and culture. It is a dynamic, ever-changing organisation, full of potential – but also full of doubts about what it can achieve, and where it should be going.

Russian architecture in Tallinn, Estonia. For the second half of the 20th century, countries of the Soviet Bloc represented the enemy for the western world.

4

A MIGHTY PROJECT

On 1 May 2004, the EU grew by about 20 per cent both in population and in land area. Then, after further expansion in January 2007, its population reached half a billion people. The European Union now has the third highest population in the world (after China and India) and the seventh largest land area (after Australia in sixth place).

What was particularly significant about the accession of new countries in 2004 and 2007, however, was not their number, or the size of their land or population, but the fact that ten of them used to belong to the Soviet Bloc – the part of the world formerly dominated by the communist government of the Soviet Union, led by Russia. For 45 years after the Second World War, the Soviet Bloc represented the enemy for western Europe, the EU and the US.

HOPES AND ANXIETIES

Fireworks, concerts, street parties and other celebrations marked the enlargement of Europe in May 2004 and January 2007. And other countries, such as Croatia, Macedonia and Turkey are hoping that soon they will be able to join Europe, too.

But in truth, these celebrations were not as spontaneous and widespread as might have been expected for such a historic event. For the EU has evolved into something altogether bigger and more ambitious than was generally envisaged by its original founders in the 1950s and 1960s. This raises many doubts and uncertainties – both among old EU member states and among the new ones. Will the EU be able to cope with the strains and stresses of such a rapid enlargement?

Street parties and celebrations in Hungary marked the country's historic accession to the European Union on 1 May 2004.

Uniting Europe

Since the beginning of history, Europe has been a complex patchwork of races, languages and nations. Europeans have often been at war with each other, constantly redrawing their boundaries. In the past, a number of attempts have been made to unite Europeans under one government.

• The Romans conquered western Europe and the lands around the Mediterranean, and ruled them as a relatively peaceful empire for 400 years.
• The French emperor Napoleon conquered and ruled much of continental western Europe, from Spain to Poland, between 1796 and 1813.
• The Germans, led by Adolf Hitler, and his Axis allies in Italy and the Balkans, ruled over a territory stretching from France to the Black Sea and eastern Russia between 1939 and 1942.

The EU is an attempt to achieve similar ends by peaceful means. It has been called 'the world's greatest peace project'.

Will the new, and comparatively poor, member states be swamped by the wealth and power of the old member states? Will jobs be taken by immigrants who are willing to work harder for less money? Will the EU become a superstate, stealing national identity and pride from individual member nations?

These and other questions make many people nervous about the future of the European Union. But while there is fear and anxiety, there is also hope and excitement. For many young Europeans, the EU offers extraordinary possibilities for travelling, studying and working abroad, learning new languages, and experiencing different cultures. In general, it is young people who are most enthusiastic about the EU, and they are its future.

5

A NEW ERA

In the early 1950s, Europe was still recovering from the devastation of the Second World War. To the founders of the EU, there were two main priorities: to nurture recovery and prosperity through international economic co-operation, and to create such strong links between European countries that such a war could never happen again.

The EU began modestly in 1951 as a co-operative venture between six nations in the trade of coal and steel. But even then, the project was driven by a greater vision of a Europe united by common goals – where freedom, security and justice could thrive, and economic and social progress could be promoted.

The EU's history dates back to the Treaty of Paris (1951) and the formal creation of the European Coal and Steel Community the following year.

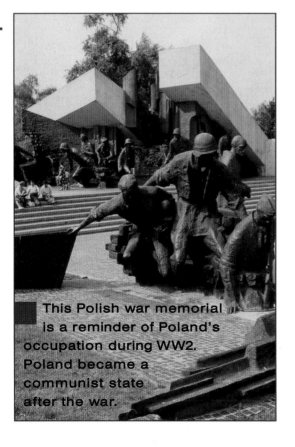

This Polish war memorial is a reminder of Poland's occupation during WW2. Poland became a communist state after the war.

BLEAK REPRESSION

The Soviet Union was a communist dictatorship, then under the ferociously repressive control of Joseph Stalin (who ruled from 1929 to 1953). All Soviet-controlled countries became communist – the State controlled all aspects of life, including work, education, sport and the arts. All property belonged to the State. People were kept under strict control by secret police and anyone caught disobeying the State, or even criticising it, was severely punished.

Under communism, life was bleak and hard for the majority of people, and prospects looked dismal. People had to queue to buy basic food. There was no incentive to start a business, to innovate or invent: the only routes to personal advancement were through the Communist Party. Then, in 1989, the world changed dramatically, as the Soviet Union began to unravel and the communist system collapsed.

A New Era

THE CAPITALIST WEST

Meanwhile, western Europe was recovering from the war, largely kick-started by a generous aid programme from the US (called the Marshall Plan) of US$13 (£7) billion between 1948 and 1953.

Compared to the communist eastern Europe, western Europe had a very different political and economic system. Here, government was (and is) based on a system of democracy whereby people choose their own rulers. The economy is based on the principle of the free market, where money, trade and jobs are regulated not by the government but by 'supply and demand' – what there is to have (supply) and what people want (demand). In contrast to the communist system (where everything is owned and run by the State), western Europe has a capitalist system, in which property, businesses and companies are owned by individuals who are free to compete with each other to make a profit. The capitalist system is not perfect, but it allows people to be creative and inventive, and to make the most of their lives. The European Union embodies these political and economic principles.

The Iron Curtain

After the Second World War, the contrast between eastern and western Europe became glaringly apparent. Many in the east wanted to escape from communist rule, but were prevented by heavily fortified borders. The long frontier dividing Europe became known as the 'Iron Curtain' – referring to both the physical border and the division in attitudes between east and west. The divide was also a defence barrier for western Europe against the Soviet Bloc – their new enemy. Both sides developed nuclear weapons and a new era (the 'Cold War') was dogged by secrecy, rivalry and mistrust.

By the 1980s, it became obvious that the communist experiment wasn't working. While the western world prospered, the Soviet Bloc remained poor and backward. The communist collapse began in Berlin in 1989, when the Berlin Wall was demolished, allowing people from the communist half of the city into the western part for the first time in nearly 30 years. Within a few years, countries across eastern Europe succeeded in winning their independence.

7

Winston Churchill, Franklin D. Roosevelt and Joseph Stalin at the Yalta Conference in 1945. At Yalta, Stalin agreed to permit free elections in eastern Europe but he later broke his promise, installing governments dominated by the Soviet Union.

Paul-Henri Spaak (1899-1972)

A leading Socialist politician, Spaak served as foreign minister and prime minister of Belgium during four decades (from the 1930s to 1960s). A long-term advocate of European integration, he also held high profile jobs as first president of the General Assembly of the United Nations, chairman of the Council for European Recovery, and secretary-general of NATO.

Key personalities of the European Union

Jean Monnet (1888-1979)

As a leading French economist, Jean Monnet was asked to draw up a plan for French economic recovery after the Second World War. He drafted first the Monnet Plan for the revitalisation of French industry, and then the Schuman Plan, which laid the foundation of the European Coal and Steel Community (ECSC), of which he was the first president (1952-55). Monnet saw the ECSC as the first step to European integration. In 1955 he formed the Action Committee for a United States of Europe.

Robert Schuman (1886-1963)

Schuman was a French lawyer and politician, who served as prime minister, then foreign minister of France in the late 1940s. In 1950, he produced the Schuman Plan (drafted by Monnet), from which the ECSC was formed in 1952. He believed that if France and Germany and other nations pooled vital resources, war would be unthinkable.

Konrad Adenauer (1876-1967)

As an opponent of the Nazis, after the war Adenauer helped form the Christian Democratic Union (CDU), which became a leading political party in West Germany. He was elected chancellor (the equivalent of prime minister in Germany) in 1949, and served until 1962, overseeing Germany's extraordinary economic revival. He was a strong supporter of a secure and united Europe, which he saw as a foundation stone of Germany's prosperity.

Jacques Delors (born 1925)

A French economist and politician, Delors served in the socialist government of President Mitterrand in the early 1980s before becoming president of the European Commission (1985-95). He steered through the Single European Act in 1986, and oversaw the transformation of the European Community (EC) into the more integrated European Union (EU) under the Maastricht Treaty of 1991.

Valéry Giscard d'Estaing (born 1926)

Giscard d'Estaing was elected president of France (1974-81) having served as finance minister in the 1960s and early 1970s. In 2001, he was appointed president of the Convention on the Future of Europe, which drew up a new EU constitution in advance of enlargement in 2004.

Romano Prodi (born 1939)

Prodi, a professor of economics, was prime minister of Italy from 1996 to 1998. As president of the EU Commission (1999-2004) he oversaw the introduction of the Euro and the EU enlargement of

2004. The former prime minister of Portugal, José Manuel Durão Barroso, succeeded Prodi as president of the EU Commission in November 2004.

During the summer months the Old Town Square in Prague is filled with tourists relaxing against the backdrop of its remarkable medieval buildings.

A NEW OPPORTUNITY

After the collapse of communism there was a huge sense of relief that the Cold War was over but also anxiety as the newly independent countries struggled to find their feet. The former communist countries began to go through rapid changes as they switched to the capitalist system. Shops filled with goods and people could travel widely – if they could afford it. Former soviet-controlled governments quickly recognised that joining the EU would help to secure their countries' future.

By 2007, a whole new generation had grown up in eastern Europe. Many young people can barely remember the communist era, but they are very much aware of its legacy, and of the precious value of freedom and independence. For older generations, memories of life under communism still remain vivid. Many agreed with Günter Verheugen, the EU's commissioner for enlargement, when he said in 2004 that the union of countries on 1 May was 'a milestone in the history of Europe... an opportunity to heal the wounds of the past.'

From coal and steel to a United Europe

The European Coal and Steel Community (ECSC) was founded by France, Germany, Italy, Belgium, the Netherlands and Luxembourg (known as 'The Six'). The ECSC agreed to merge coal and steel industries under one authority and to remove barriers that inhibited trade. In 1957, The Six signed the Treaty of Rome to create a trading zone for all products, goods and labour, called the European Economic Community (EEC). In 1967, the ECSC, EEC and the European Atomic Energy Community (EURATOM) were combined to form the European Community (EC).

Over time, more countries joined the EC: Denmark, Ireland and the United Kingdom (1973); Greece (1981); Portugal and Spain (1986); Austria, Finland and Sweden (1995). Each enlargement was deeply controversial, with strong arguments on both sides.

The European Union (EU) was formed with the Maastricht Treaty in 1991, which laid the foundations for Economic and Monetary Union (EMU). Ten new countries joined in 2004 – Cyprus, the Czech Republic, Estonia, Hungary, Latvia, Lithuania, Malta, Poland, Slovakia and Slovenia. In 2007, Romania and Bulgaria joined. Croatia, Macedonia and Turkey are still waiting.

9

MAP OF EUROPE

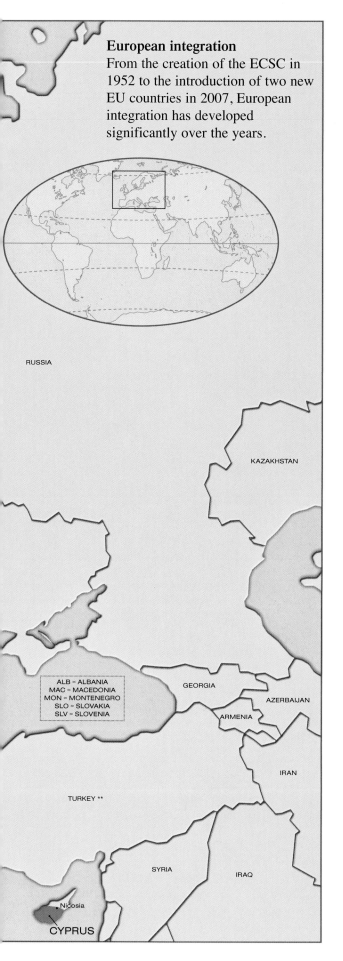

European integration

From the creation of the ECSC in 1952 to the introduction of two new EU countries in 2007, European integration has developed significantly over the years.

RUSSIA

KAZAKHSTAN

ALB = ALBANIA
MAC = MACEDONIA
MON = MONTENEGRO
SLO = SLOVAKIA
SLV = SLOVENIA

GEORGIA

AZERBAIJAN

ARMENIA

IRAN

TURKEY **

SYRIA

IRAQ

Nicosia

CYPRUS

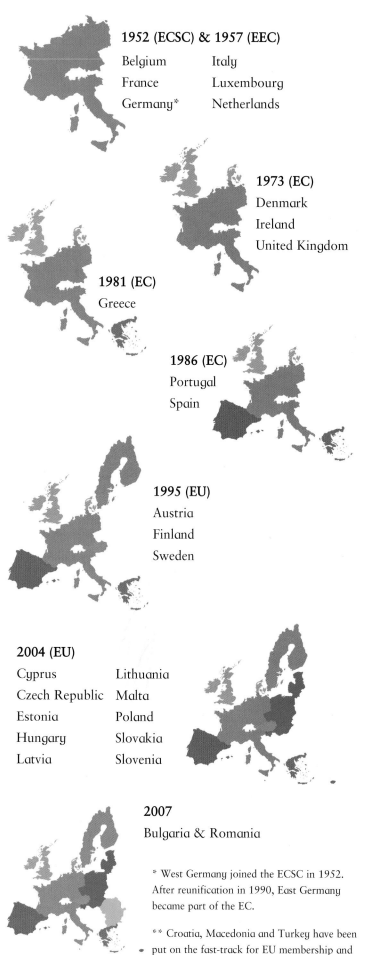

1952 (ECSC) & 1957 (EEC)

Belgium	Italy
France	Luxembourg
Germany*	Netherlands

1973 (EC)

Denmark

Ireland

United Kingdom

1981 (EC)

Greece

1986 (EC)

Portugal

Spain

1995 (EU)

Austria

Finland

Sweden

2004 (EU)

Cyprus	Lithuania
Czech Republic	Malta
Estonia	Poland
Hungary	Slovakia
Latvia	Slovenia

2007

Bulgaria & Romania

* West Germany joined the ECSC in 1952. After reunification in 1990, East Germany became part of the EC.

** Croatia, Macedonia and Turkey have been put on the fast-track for EU membership and hope to join at the next stage.

11

(1) BELGIUM
Joined ECSC: 1952
Capital: Brussels
Population: 10.29 million
Area: 30,520 sq km
Currency: Euro
Languages: French, Dutch, German
GDP per capita*: $29,200
NATO member

---

(2) FRANCE
Joined ECSC: 1952
Capital: Paris
Population: 60.18 million
Area: 543,965 sq km
Currency: Euro
Languages: French, Breton, Basque
GDP per capita: $26,000
NATO member

---

(3) GERMANY
Joined ECSC: 1952
Capital: Berlin
Population: 82.4 million
Area: 357,868 sq km
Currency: Euro
Language: German
GDP per capita: $26,200
NATO member

12

---

(4) ITALY
Joined ECSC: 1952
Capital: Rome
Population: 58.0 million
Area: 301,245 sq km
Currency: Euro
Languages: Italian, German, French
GDP per capita: $25,100
NATO member

---

(5) LUXEMBOURG
Joined ECSC: 1952
Capital: Luxembourg
Population: 0.45 million
Area: 2,587 sq km
Currency: Euro
Languages: Letzeburghish, French,
German
GDP per capita: $48,900
NATO member

---

(6) NETHERLANDS
Joined ECSC: 1952
Capital: Amsterdam
Population: 16.15 million
Area: 41,526 sq km
Currency: Euro
Language: Dutch
GDP per capita: $27,200
NATO member

---

(7) DENMARK
Joined EC: 1973
Capital: Copenhagen
Population: 5.38 million
Area: 43,075 sq km
Currency: Danish Krone
Language: Danish
GDP per capita: $28,900
NATO member

---

(8) IRELAND
Joined EC: 1973
Capital: Dublin
Population: 3.92 million
Area: 70,282 sq km
Currency: Euro
Languages: English, Irish
GDP per capita: $29,300

---

(9) UNITED KINGDOM
Joined EC: 1973
Capital: London
Population: 60.09 million
Area: 242,535 sq km
Currency: Pound sterling
Languages: English, Welsh
GDP per capita: $25,500
NATO member

---

(10) GREECE
Joined EC: 1981
Capital: Athens
Population: 10.67 million
Area: 131,957 sq km
Currency: Euro
Language: Greek
GDP per capita: $19,100
NATO member

---

(11) PORTUGAL
Joined EC: 1986
Capital: Lisbon
Population: 10.10 million
Area: 88,940 sq km
Currency: Euro
Language: Portuguese
GDP per capita: $19,400
NATO member

---

(12) SPAIN
Joined EC: 1986
Capital: Madrid
Population: 40.22 million
Area: 504,782 sq km
Currency: Euro
Languages: Spanish, Catalan,
Galician, Basque
GDP per capita: $21,200
NATO member

---

(13) AUSTRIA
Joined EU: 1995
Capital: Vienna
Population: 8.19 million
Area: 83,855 sq km
Currency: Euro
Language: German
GDP per capita: $27,900

---

(14) FINLAND
Joined EU: 1995
Capital: Helsinki
Population: 5.19 million
Area: 338,145 sq km
Currency: Euro
Languages: Finnish, Swedish, Lapp
GDP per capita: $25,800

---

(15) SWEDEN
Joined EU: 1995
Capital: Stockholm
Population: 8.88 million
Area: 449,964 sq km
Currency: Swedish Krona
Languages: Swedish, Finnish, Lapp
GDP per capita: $26,000

⑯ REPUBLIC OF CYPRUS (South Only)
Joined EU: 2004
Capital: Nicosia
Population: 0.66 million
Area: 5,828 sq km
Currency: Cypriot pound
Language: Greek
GDP per capita: $20,100

⑰ CZECH REPUBLIC
Joined EU: 2004
Capital: Prague
Population: 10.25 million
Area: 78,864 sq km
Currency: Koruna
Languages: Czech, German
GDP per capita: $15,300
NATO member

⑱ ESTONIA
Joined EU: 2004
Capital: Tallinn
Population: 1.14 million
Area: 45,227 sq km
Currency: Kroon
Languages: Estonian, Russian
GDP per capita: $11,000
NATO member

⑲ HUNGARY
Joined EU: 2004
Capital: Budapest
Population: 10.05 million
Area: 93,030 sq km
Currency: Forint
Language: Hungarian
GDP per capita: $13,300
NATO member

⑳ LATVIA
Joined EU: 2004
Capital: Riga
Population: 2.35 million
Area: 64,589 sq km
Currency: Lat
Languages: Latvian, Russian
GDP per capita: $8,900
NATO member

㉑ LITHUANIA
Joined EU: 2004
Capital: Vilnius
Population: 3.60 million
Area: 65,300 sq km
Currency: Litas
Languages: Lithuanian, Russian, Polish
GDP per capita: $8,400
NATO member

㉒ MALTA
Joined EU: 2004
Capital: Valletta
Population: 0.4 million
Area: 316 sq km
Currency: Maltese Lire
Languages: Maltese, English, Italian
GDP per capita: $17,200

㉓ POLAND
Joined EU: 2004
Capital: Warsaw
Population: 38.62 million
Area: 312,683 sq km
Currency: Zloty
Languages: Polish, German
GDP per capita: $9,700
NATO member

㉔ SLOVAKIA
Joined EU: 2004
Capital: Bratislava
Population: 5.43 million
Area: 49,036 sq km
Currency: Slovak Koruna
Languages: Slovak, Hungarian, Czech
GDP per capita: $12,400
NATO member

* GDP per capita means Gross Domestic Product per person in the population (see p47) shown in US dollars.

㉕ SLOVENIA
Joined EU: 2004
Capital: Ljubljana
Population: 1.94 million
Area: 20,253 sq km
Currency: Euro
Languages: Slovene, Serbo-Croat, Hungarian, Italian
GDP per capita: $19,200
NATO member

㉖ BULGARIA
Joined EU: 2007
Capital: Sofia
Population: 7.8 million
Area: 110,994 sq km
Currency: Lev
Language: Bulgarian
GDP per capita: $3,450
NATO member

㉗ ROMANIA
Joined EU: 2007
Capital: Bucharest
Population: 21.6 million
Area: 238,391 sq km
Currency: Leu
Language: Romanian
GDP per capita: $3,830
NATO member

13

WHY ENLARGEMENT?

By the end of the 20th century, the European Union contained 15 countries, all of which ranked among the top 50 most prosperous nations in the world. These countries were edging slowly along the tricky path of increased integration. The 15 could have remained a comfortable club of wealthy nations. But in Athens in 2003, they agreed to take on ten new countries, most of which were poorer than themselves. And by 2007, the EU had increased to 27 countries, with another three hoping to join. The process was costly and would create a very different kind of EU. Why would they want to risk this disruption?

Former Latvian prime minister, Andris Berzins (left) with members of his cabinet during a government meeting in the capital Riga.

SUPPORT AND SECURITY

The answer lay in the fact that the world had changed dramatically since the early days of European integration. The Cold War had ended and the formerly Soviet-controlled countries of eastern Europe now found themselves in no-man's land – between Russia on the one hand and the EU on the other. They valued their new-found independence, but feared being alone in a rapidly changing world. They saw the EU as a safe haven for their fledgling democratic systems and free-market economies, providing both support and a vision for the future. Referendums showed strong approval for joining the EU, from 67 per cent of the vote in Latvia and Estonia to 92 per cent in Slovakia.

For its part, the EU saw a historic opportunity to bring eastern Europe onto its side. In 1993, shortly after the collapse of the Soviet Union, the EU summit meeting (European Council) in Copenhagen declared its willingness to accept any eastern European country that wanted to join, and eight ex-communist countries had successfully applied by 1996.

Audi TT car bodies in the assembly hall of an Audi factory at Györ, Hungary.

ECONOMIC GROWTH

The EU nations were also keen to get eastern Europe on board – the east offered a huge new market for EU products and had a large, skilled labour force producing goods at less cost. It is estimated that this new market will add nearly £2 billion to the income of Britain alone. Eastern Europe welcomed EU investment which brought jobs, new technology and rapid economic growth. For example, during the 1990s, factories were set up in Slovenia by the French car manufacturer Renault and the German pharmaceutical company Bayer. Even before it joined the EU, Slovenia had become wealthier (in terms of GDP per capita) than Greece and Portugal.

Cyprus and Malta do not have a communist background and had rather different cases for EU membership. Both are small and geographically on the edges of Europe. The EU now gives them greater security, a higher status in the world and, above all, the advantages of belonging to a large, single market. For, in terms of trade, the EU market for goods and services now exceeds the US in both size and wealth.

15

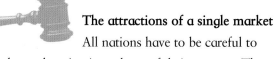

The attractions of a single market

All nations have to be careful to control the trade going in and out of their country. They might also charge taxes or customs duties to raise money and to protect their own industries from competition from cheaper foreign products.

To make trade easier, two countries might scrap their import duties, allowing trade to cross freely between the two countries and creating a 'single market' for other nations. During the 1980s, the creation of a single market was an important goal for the EU. The Single European Act (1986) introduced the Single Market in 1993, which applied to goods, capital (such as investment in industries), services (such as banking) and people (who could potentially live and work anywhere in the EU).

The EU will only become a perfect single market when all trading conditions are consistent. The US is an example of a near-perfect single market with one language, one currency, common standards and a uniform legal system.

A worker at a food-processing factory in Hungary prepares locally-produced green peas for canning.

CLUB BENEFITS

The EU's Single Market permits manufacturers and traders both within the EU and abroad to treat all EU nations as one. On a practical level, it means that trade can pass far more easily across borders. Before joining the EU, Hungarian lorry drivers had to wait in long queues at the customs border with Austria and paid large sums of money on customs duties. Now many of these procedures have been scrapped.

Since the introduction of the Single Market, three million jobs in the UK are now linked to the export of goods and services to the European Union. Now, well over half of British trade is with the EU. New members of the EU expect similar advantages from the Single Market.

Preparations for accession

Before any country can join the EU, it has to meet certain standards. The 12 countries who joined between 2004 and 2007 were required to have: stable institutions that would guarantee democracy, human rights and the protection of minority groups; a fully functioning market economy; the capacity to cope with the economic pressures of EU membership; and the ability to take on all the obligations of membership.

The former communist countries (which in the early 1990s had little experience in democracy, and inefficient industries) had to make radical changes to overhaul their standards in trade, banking, law and the environment, and had to make tough decisions on financial reform. In the 1990s, an EU welfare programme called 'Phare' was set up to assist the accession countries. In 2006, for example, Bulgaria and Romania got about €1.5 billion in pre-accession aid to help reforms and to close the wealth gap between them and other EU members.

FEARS, DOUBTS AND COSTS

Not all countries think that the EU is a good idea – the Norwegians rejected proposals to join in 1973 and 1994; Switzerland withdrew its application in 1992; and a referendum in Malta brought only a 54 per cent vote in favour of membership.

In the last decade, many eastern Europeans felt nervous about joining the EU. Their national identities were bruised and fragile after decades of ruthless domination by the Soviet Union. With the prospect of accession, they feared that they might be swamped by another alien culture – that of the west.

In 2004, many people in the 15 existing EU nations doubted whether enlargement was wise. They remembered the difficulties that Germany has faced since the reunification of East and West Germany in the 1990s, and feared that absorbing the former countries of eastern Europe would bring similar difficulties. They also felt that eastern Europe – as poor contributors to the EU's total economic output – would be a burden on the EU's finances.

The question of EU membership remains a key political issue in Switzerland.

Enlargement comes at a cost, for both existing members and new members. For example, the EU spent around €67 billion on the 2004 enlargement. But this cost is relatively small in comparison to what the EU economy gains as a result. While the EU's average economic growth has been 2% a year, with the accession of Bulgaria and Romania, the rate is expected to increase to 2.7% in 2007, because these new countries are developing so rapidly.

Why do we want to enlarge the EU when countries elsewhere are struggling to become independent?

Just as the EU was seeking to expand its membership, other groups of nations were falling apart. After the Soviet Bloc collapsed in the early 1990s, Yugoslavia broke up into a patchwork of warring states. One of these was Slovenia – now a member of the EU, 12 years after gaining independence.

Loss of independence is a dilemma for all EU nations. Countries have their unique history, languages and traditions. Outside the EU, governments are free to make all their laws, and to control their trade and economy; as EU members, they have to sacrifice some of this power.

The EU demands a balancing act. If nations give up a part of their independence and sovereignty, they need to feel that they are getting something in return. By joining the EU, they gain the security and prosperity that comes with being part of a powerful union and trading bloc.

Some people see the future of the EU as a single state with its own government, constitution and currency. Others believe that Europe should concentrate on being a successful trading club of independent nations. The amount of power handed to a centralised EU government is likely to remain a burning issue for many years to come.

The debating chamber (the 'hemicycle') of the European Parliament in Strasbourg. The European Parliament has monthly sessions in Strasbourg, for final votes, while all preparatory meetings take place in Brussels.

POLITICAL ADVANTAGE

With a total of 27 member states, the EU has become a more powerful force in the world. The EU now represents a political force similar to that of Russia and China. And if EU member states combined, they would have the world's largest economy by GDP.

Enlargement also helped to redefine the EU. By adding so many new members, the political balance within the group has shifted. Existing members saw their own power diluted: instead of being one in a club of 15, they became one in a club of 27. Many of those who want to see Europe become a more centralised political unit (a 'United States of Europe') saw enlargement as a set-back. But those who prefer to see the EU purely as a trading bloc, viewed enlargement more favourably and welcomed a wider distribution of power. The new nations, they argue, are less likely to give up their hard-won independence by handing over their sovereignty to the EU; and France and Germany will be less able to dominate the EU, as they have in the past.

The Eurosceptics

Many Europeans feel that the idea of a united Europe simply will not work.

Doubters and critics have been given the label 'Eurosceptics' (the word 'sceptic' means someone who doubts or mistrusts beliefs, ideas and people). The Eurosceptics' doubts centre on a number of issues:

• In trying to standardise all aspects of trade for the Single Market, the EU meddles too much in the business of individual nations.
• The EU appears to want to draw ever more power away from national governments and towards the centralised EU institutions. In so doing, the EU conflicts with national sovereignty, independence, and age-old feelings of national identity.
• The EU is run by career politicians and bureaucrats, and is not properly democratic.
• The EU uses its members' money wastefully, and its spending is not properly monitored.

The opposite of a Eurosceptic is a 'Europhile' – someone who is an enthusiastic supporter of the European project.

A NEW SUPERPOWER?

There is only really one superpower in the world today: the US. China and Russia have the potential to develop into superpowers. And so, too, does the European Union. The EU now has about 11% of the world's population (the third largest continent in terms of population after Asia and Africa). Its economy is also growing fast. But a superpower needs a strong central government, and it also needs a strong army. The EU has neither of these.

Enlargement celebrations on 1 May 2004 outside the European Parliament in Brussels. In 2007, another two members joined.

THE UNITED STATES OF EUROPE

The idea of a 'United States of Europe' is not new. In fact a number of people, including Winston Churchill and Jean Monnet, expressed this as a distant dream after the Second World War.

In reality, the EU is a long way from achieving this goal – and the accession of 12 new nations in 2004 and 2007 may have made this dream more remote. Many oppose the 'United States' idea; but the possibility should not be ruled out for the future.

The EU already has many aspects of a country, if not a superpower. It has a parliament, a civil service, a court of justice and its own currency. If the new constitution is ever approved, it will also soon have its own president. The EU also has a large presence on the world stage: at the United Nations (UN); at meetings of the G-8 (a club of the world's leading industrial nations); in negotiations with the World Trade Organisation (WTO); and in agreements with Russia and other countries of the former Soviet Bloc.

RELATIONSHIPS WITH THE US

Although the US primarily sees the EU as a trading partner, America has shown exceptional support for Europe over the years – providing vital military assistance in the two World Wars, a generous aid programme in the 1940s and 1950s and continued military support through NATO.

Yet, America receives two conflicting signals from the EU. Some member nations (notably France) want to build up the EU as a counterweight to growing US power. Other nations (such as the UK and countries of eastern Europe) see the US as an essential ally.

The EU depends heavily on the US for its military defence, through NATO. Following the collapse of Yugoslavia in the 1990s, NATO forces were called upon to enforce peace in Bosnia in 1995, and Kosovo in 1999, where they received extensive US military assistance. Meanwhile, in an effort to placate the fears of Russia about the growth of NATO, a Partnership for Peace was established in 1994 – joining NATO with many countries formerly associated with the Soviet Union.

The Euro

Until 2002, if you travelled around Europe you would have to change currency every time you crossed a border: Francs in France, Marks in Germany, Lire in Italy and Schillings in Austria. These currencies all looked different and had rates of exchange that fluctuated, making it even harder for manufacturers and traders who were buying and selling goods abroad.

In 2002, twelve (of the then 15) member states adopted the Euro after completing tough financial reforms to bring their currencies in line with one another (a process called 'convergence'). Despite warnings of widespread chaos, the new currency was introduced with remarkable ease. However, despite Slovenia adopting the Euro in 2007, since enlargement, the Euro is now the currency of just under half the EU states, and is likely to remain so for some time. The Euro is managed by the European Central Bank, based in Frankfurt.

US president, George W Bush (right) with his former secretary of defence, Donald Rumsfeld (centre), and his former deputy secretary of defence, Paul Wolfowitz (left), at a meeting at the Pentagon, Washington.

British prime minister, Tony Blair, with Russian president, Vladimir Putin, during a foreign office press conference in London.

NATO and the EU

The North Atlantic Treaty Organisation (NATO) was founded in 1949 as a military alliance between the US, Canada, most western European countries and Turkey. Its primary task was to provide a counterbalance to the power of the Soviet Bloc. NATO would go to the assistance of any members if they felt under attack.

After the collapse of the Soviet Union, many former communist countries were anxious to secure their defences by allying themselves to the west. Ten of the recent 12 accession countries in eastern Europe have joined NATO in recent decades – much to the alarm of Russia. Now, 21 of the 27 EU nations are NATO members. The six exceptions are Ireland, Austria, Finland, Sweden, Cyprus and Malta.

The EU is closely bonded to NATO but it would also like to develop its own European Defence Force. Several factors make this difficult: the US remains an essential part of European defence, providing overwhelming military power; the EU is reluctant to finance its defences to superpower level; and the EU already finds it difficult to agree on foreign policy.

THE IRAQ WAR

A number of issues have strained the relationship between the EU and the US in recent years. For example, although the EU approved of the Kyoto Protocol on climate change, the US refused. There is also an ongoing dispute over the EU's reluctance to introduce genetically modified (GM) crops and food, most of which come from the US. In 2004, the EU raised import duties against US goods. This was in retaliation for the US practice of giving subsidies, in the form of tax breaks, which give an unfair trading advantage to exporters such as Boeing and Microsoft.

But relationships between Europe and the US have really become strained since the Iraq War of 2003 and the subsequent US-led occupation. Europe has been divided by the issue – the governments of France and Germany opposed the US-led plan to invade Iraq, while the British government actively supported it, along with the governments of the eastern European countries, such as Poland and Estonia (in general, eastern European countries are pro-US, in recognition of America's support against their former communist regimes). Increasing doubts about the reasons behind the US invasion of Iraq have enhanced tensions between EU countries even further.

The Iraq war has revealed divisions within Europe, and pointed to the difficulty the EU will always have in agreeing about foreign policy and military action. Until it can resolve such divisions and speak and act with one voice, it can never be a superpower.

A SUPERCURRENCY

The EU's relationship with the US is not simply a question of defence, however. The EU is closely linked to the US in a number of areas, including trade, the exchange of technology and ideas, professional training, culture and entertainment.

The EU (along with countries such as China and Japan) invests heavily in the US, helping to sustain the US economy. Many countries choose to hold their national reserves in US dollars, but if support for the dollar weakens, the international community may look for another currency in which to hold their reserves – in just the same way as it switched from British pounds sterling to US dollars in the early 20th century. It is possible that they may switch to the Euro, further boosting the position of the EU in the world.

Other economic and political blocs

There are several other economic and political blocs, although none share quite the same level of cohesion as the EU. They include:

The African Union – Founded in 2002 (to succeed the Organisation of African Unity), the African Union protects the interests of the African states, with the exception of Morocco. It aims to promote democracy and human rights, resolve disputes and encourage development (particularly through foreign investment).

CIS: The Commonwealth of Independent States

After the collapse of the Soviet Union, 12 of its 15 member states clubbed together as the CIS, and formed a free trade zone. They include Belarus and the Ukraine, as well as the Central Asian states such as Uzbekistan. Russia is the dominant force, and is responsible for defence. The three exceptions are the Baltic States (Estonia, Latvia and Lithuania) which have joined the EU.

The Commonwealth of Nations – Previously called the British Commonwealth, this is a group of more than 50 countries (mostly former members of the British Empire). It serves as a forum for discussion of common issues.

NAFTA: The North American Free Trade Agreement

Signed in 1992, NAFTA was designed to eliminate all tariffs and trade barriers between Canada, the US and Mexico within 15 years. Prior to the 2004 enlargement of the EU, it was the world's largest trading bloc.

OPEC: Organisation of Petroleum-Exporting Countries

This economically powerful group meets regularly to discuss oil production and the price of oil. It includes the big oil producers, such as Saudi Arabia and the Middle Eastern states, and Indonesia, Nigeria and Venezuela. However, the group excludes Russia, potentially the world's biggest oil producer after OPEC.

The value of national currencies fluctuates according to the financial market. The US dollar has been the dominant world currency for over 100 years.

RUNNING THE EU

Operating an organisation that represents half a billion people and 27 countries is not an easy task. Over the years, the EU has developed institutions that deal with all aspects of government, based mainly in Brussels (the 'capital' of the EU), Strasbourg and Luxembourg. How will these institutions stand up to the pressures and demands of an enlarged Union? Now that there are 27 member states, free discussion around a table has become almost impossible. If ministers take just three minutes each to declare their point of view, a meeting will last an hour and 20 minutes even before any kind of discussion can begin.

RUNNING THE EU GOVERNMENT

The EU has four main institutions:

The **European Commission** (based in Brussels) is essentially the EU's civil service and policy-maker, with a staff of about 20,000.

The **Council of Ministers** (also based in Brussels) is the main decision-making body of the EU. It brings together government ministers from the member states to make decisions on key issues.

The **European Parliament** (meeting in Brussels and Strasbourg) is a body of members (MEPs) elected by constituents in their home country. Although the Parliament is not as powerful as national governments, it is having an increasing influence on decision-making within the EU.

The **European Court of Justice** (based in Luxembourg) ensures that the legal framework of the EU is upheld, and that justice throughout the EU is conducted evenly.

Statue of a woman holding the Euro symbol, outside the European Parliament in Brussels.

POWER AND RESPONSIBILITY

Although the EU may appear to be like a government, it does not have a fully democratic basis: policy is made by appointed commissioners; decisions are made by government ministers representing individual nations; and elected MEPs only have limited powers. This poses a problem if the EU is really going to become a United States of Europe.

Member states of the EU have indirect control over the policies of the Union, but the EU also only has indirect control over the behaviour of its members. The EU has produced thousands of rules but does not possess all the powers it needs to ensure that they are carried out.

In Britain, for instance, greengrocers have been prosecuted for selling fruit and vegetables in traditional weights of pounds and ounces, instead of using metric kilograms and grams, as directed by the EU. On a larger scale, EU countries are supposed to keep their budget deficits to within three per cent of GDP. Both France and Germany recently broke these limits. Other EU members could have punished them by imposing fines, but clearly this would only have made the financial difficulties of France and Germany worse; instead, the rules were simply suspended. This lack of consistency in imposing EU rules can be highly irritating to those who obey them – often at the cost of considerable hardship and expense to themselves.

Cyprus: still divided

The island of Cyprus has two communities: Greek Cypriots (81 per cent) in the south and Turkish Cypriots (19 per cent) in the north. When the island became independent from British colonial rule in 1960, tensions flared up between the two communities. In 1974 Turkey sent in troops, taking 40 per cent of the land and dividing the island in two – only the Greek, southern half was recognised by the international community. Cyprus applied to join the EU in 1990, and the EU declared that it would accept all the island if it agreed to unite. A vote was held in April 2004 – the Turkish community (desperate to end their isolation and poverty) voted for unity but the Greeks voted against it. So, only the internationally-recognised Greek, southern part of the island joined the EU in 2004.

THE CONSTITUTION

In June 2004, the EU agreed a draft constitution designed to act as a framework for its operation. The formation of this document was led by the former president of France, Valéry Giscard d'Estaing.

The draft constitution defines the powers of the EU and the roles of the EU institutions. The document also summarises the main treaties agreed by the EU, and it attempts to streamline the EU institutions to improve decision-making during the process of enlargement.

However, although the draft document was agreed in 2004 by the EU's 25 nations, France and the Netherlands voted against the constitution when they held referendums in 2005. This was a major blow because the constitution has to be agreed by all member states before it can come into force. The debate is expected to emerge again in 2007, however, when Germany takes over the EU presidency. France and the Netherlands are also due to have elections in 2007, which may change political views.

Members of the European Parliament vote during a meeting in Strasbourg.

Shouldn't we all just speak English?

The EU now has 23 official languages. Since 2004, the number of official translators at the European Commission has almost quadrupled, from 1,300 to around 4,000. The EU is still struggling to find translators to convert Maltese into Lithuanian, and Slovenian into Finnish and the number of language combinations for interpretation is becoming more and more restricted as the EU gets bigger.

In reality, the EU's common language is English, which is taught in schools in virtually all the EU countries. Almost all EU officials speak fluent English. Some people argue that it would make sense to make English the official language. This situation irritates a number of member states, particularly France – French was one of the main EU languages prior to UK membership in 1973. France also views the UK as a reluctant member of the EU.

Eurosceptics complain that the constitution enshrines the idea of a United States of Europe, or at least a Federal Europe, at the expense of national sovereignty. Others feel that the constitution still safeguards key areas of national sovereignty, establishing a 'group of nations', rather than a superstate.

Either way, the constitution has become the first big challenge of the enlarged Europe. Some think that a new constitution could still be approved by 2009, but others are more pessimistic. And if member states can't agree on the constitution, how will they ever agree on major issues that confront the EU?

The European Parliament is mostly based in Brussels, where committee meetings are held to discuss the intricacies of legislation and a full assembly is held for two days every month.

STRUCTURAL CHANGES

The draft constitution provides for two important innovations. It suggests that the EU should be led by a president, elected by Council members to serve for up to five years; this office would replace the six-month rotating presidency of the Council of Ministers. The EU would also have its own foreign minister (a role currently performed by two commissioners). The idea is that these two posts would help to present a more unified image of the EU to the rest of the world.

Decisions at the Council of Ministers have to be passed either unanimously or by majority vote. To speed up decision-making in an enlarged EU, the new constitution proposes that the number of policy areas where majority voting may be applied should be extended. Not all members are happy that key areas of government, such as immigration and social policy, might now be overruled by a majority vote.

The draft constitution also proposes changes at the European Commission, to address the concern that larger countries may be outvoted by smaller countries. Instead of every member state having a commissioner with equal voting rights, the constitution proposes some voting commissioners and some non-voting commissioners to be rotated on an equal basis.

The Common Agricultural Policy

One of the most controversial EU issues is the Common Agricultural Policy (CAP). Each year, the EU spends about 45 per cent of its total budget to protect its farmers against foreign competition, by guaranteeing the price of farm products and providing subsidies.

In the 1980s, a massive oversupply in subsidised products resulted in stockpiles of unwanted commodities, such as the so-called 'wine lakes' and 'butter mountains'. More careful funding has since prevented such excesses, but the cost of the CAP can still appear excessive and wasteful. It can also appear grossly unfair to countries of the Third World that are unable to compete. The cost of the CAP is gradually being reduced, but any reduction to CAP payouts is fiercely resisted by farmers – many of whom would go bankrupt if the subsidies were removed.

In the new accession countries, a comparatively large proportion of income comes from agriculture. The cost of supporting eastern European farms could have bankrupted the EU, so the EU initially distributed just 25 per cent of the CAP subsidy, and is gradually increasing payments to farmers who have fully modernised.

INITIAL HITCHES

Before the draft constitution could be adopted, its contents first had to be agreed. There were numerous sticking points, such as changes in voting rights and references to religion – seven Catholic countries (including Italy and Poland) pressed for a reference to the 'Christian roots of Europe' in the constitution. However, the EU rejected these requests referring only to the 'cultural, religious and humanist' traditions of Europe.

The question of how the constitution should be ratified is also controversial. Some believe that, on an issue as important as the EU constitution, a referendum should allow the public to say whether they agree. Others believe that referendums reflect current attitudes to governments more than well-informed judgements about the issue involved. There are enough Eurosceptics in Europe to suggest that other countries might also say 'no' to the constitution. And unless all countries agree, the constitution cannot be passed.

27

'Food mountains' caused by an oversupply in subsidised products were a major focus of criticism of the Common Agricultural Policy in the 1980s.

Fishermen on the coast of the Baltic Sea in Dyiwnow, Poland. The EU's Common Fisheries Policy (2003) aims to provide sustainable fishing and a healthy marine environment.

TWO-SPEED EUROPE

It is possible that the diversity of EU member states might lead to a 'two-speed Europe'. In the fast lane will be the countries that are enthusiastic to forge ahead with European unity, such as adoption of the Euro and the EU constitution. In the slow lane will be those that remain half-hearted about the project.

Britain has often been accused of being an awkward partner in the EU, having opted out of the single currency and issues of social policy introduced by the Maastricht Treaty in 1991. The slow lane might also include some of the new members who are concerned about their sovereignty. At some point, the European institutions may have to decide to what extent those in the slow lane should be allowed to participate in the decision-making processes. It is certainly hard to see how a 'two-speed Europe' can work within the current framework.

Environmental issues

Air pollution and water pollution do not respect national frontiers. Poisonous fumes from a factory can cause great damage in a neighbouring country, and polluted rivers can cross borders.

Pollution is an area in which the EU has shown great strength. Considerable concern was expressed about the pollution produced by the old industries of the former communist countries. Indeed, millions of Euros were spent in these countries to tackle environmental problems before accession in 2004 and 2007. Environmental issues are also closely linked to economic matters. This is particularly the case in fishing – the seas around the EU have seen dramatic declines in fish populations, due to overfishing. The EU has imposed strict limits on fishing, but this remains a contentious issue since many trawling fleets have gone out of business as a result.

28

WHO WINS? WHO LOSES?

While the EU has many benefits, there are always going to be those that fear for a loss of independence and national sovereignty. The EU is certainly not perfect. Who wins and who loses depends on whom you ask and where they live. But the EU can boast some extraordinary successes. Some 30 years ago, Spain, Portugal and Greece were all relatively poor countries, living under dictatorships. Now they are modern, prosperous, democratic countries – a state of affairs directly linked to being part of the EU. Many of the new accession countries hope to share the same kind of success.

FUNDS, SUBSIDIES AND CONTRIBUTIONS

Running the EU is a huge – and expensive – task. The EU currently spends about €120 billion a year. All member countries make a contribution to the costs, roughly in proportion to the size of their economies. Germany is the largest contributor to EU funds, because it has the largest EU economy (the fifth largest in the world after China, the USA, India and Japan).

Each country receives some money back in the form of subsidies; the biggest subsidies go to the poorer countries. Some countries give more than they receive (net contributors), others receive more than they give. The two largest areas of spending for the EU are the CAP (see page 27) and structural funds (which cover major projects such as transport development, industry and the environment, and regional development funds directed towards areas in need of regeneration).

The costs of German reunification in 1990 have been a heavy burden to the German economy. Despite this, Germany still remains the main contributor to the EU budget.

Almost all of the 2004 and 2007 accession countries (excluding Slovenia and Cyprus) are poor enough to qualify for EU assistance. In 2005, for example, the ten countries which joined the EU in 2004 received about €4 billion more from the EU than they paid into the budget.

The Commission wants to increase the contributions made by member states – a move that six net contributors, the UK, France, Germany, the Netherlands, Austria and Sweden, are resisting.

COSTS AND BENEFITS

EU membership is a major financial commitment, and politicians have to play a delicate game to keep their country supportive of the EU. Billions of Euros have been pledged for infrastructure in the new member states, but in other ways, the EU has been less generous – the reduced CAP subsidies for accession countries, for example, mean that many eastern European farmers may lose their livelihood.

The EU has also not lived up to its promises in the job market. When the EU enlarged in 2004, many of the existing EU countries introduced restrictions making it harder for eastern Europeans to work in the west – and, in effect, making them feel like second-class EU citizens. There are gains and losses as people move to work abroad. Those that can travel tend to be skilled and educated. Young Polish doctors can earn £5,000 a year in Poland; but they can earn £60,000 in the UK. However, such skilled workers are precisely the people needed in their home countries to build their prosperity.

National governments versus the EU

Independence gives a country the right to choose how it runs its affairs. It can choose how to run the government, how to make and apply its own laws, what taxes everyone should pay, and so on. The EU also has its own set of rules and regulations. With the drive towards greater European unity, national governments have had to hand over some of their power and sovereignty to the EU.

Today, nearly half of all the legislation passed by the British parliament originates in Brussels. EU law also takes precedence over national laws – if you feel that justice is not being done in your own country, you can take your case to the European Court of Justice, which can overrule judgements made by national courts. Handing over power to the EU has to be carefully negotiated – a nation will only hand over its control if it can be certain that the EU is competent to use it, and if it receives some benefit in return.

University students during a graduation ceremony in Tal'Qorq, Malta. Graduates in Malta can look forward to the possibility of using their qualifications to work elsewhere in the EU.

A production line for Volkswagen Polo cars in Bratislava, Slovakia.

SHIFTING FORTUNES

In the last ten years, many countries in western Europe have experienced a recession, with rising unemployment and stagnating economies. Some people blamed this on the introduction of the Euro, others on the high costs of labour and employment in many of the old EU nations.

Although the recession is lifting, EU enlargement in 2004 made the situation worse in some areas. Some manufacturers set up new factories in eastern Europe at the expense of workers in the west. But eastern Europeans did not have all the advantages. As their industries had to conform to EU standards, their factories had to invest in new equipment – and this extra cost was passed on to consumers. Countries were also unable to subsidise certain industries. Hungary, for instance, is no longer allowed to give tax breaks to foreign industries investing in new factories. Without the offer of these tax breaks, large foreign companies have begun to look elsewhere.

Can one size fit all?

A common complaint about the EU is that it meddles too much in the lives of its citizens, by imposing countless rules and restrictions. For example, numerous small food producers across Europe have struggled to meet the demands of EU regulations on hygiene, workplace safety, labelling and packaging – which often involves buying expensive equipment, and sometimes causes them to go out of business.

The task of the EU officials, on the other hand, is to ensure that, in the Single Market, competition is fair. A company may produce kitchen knives, for example, in the safest way possible; but another company may be able to produce them more cheaply by disregarding health and safety regulations. This is not just unfair to the workers, but unfair competition.

The EU Commission also wants to see taxes standardised, or 'harmonised', across the EU, since these have a direct effect upon prices and spending power. But national governments argue that they need to control their own taxes to be able to fine-tune their economies. EU standardisation is a constant tussle between the quest for uniformity, and the need to protect freedoms, independence and individuality.

THE WIDER WORLD

EU policy also has an impact abroad. The CAP subsidies for European farming contravenes the principles of the World Trade Organisation (WTO) on fair international trade, and distorts the market for Third World producers.

Yet in other ways the EU is extremely generous. Although budget cuts are on the horizon, the EU is currently the world's largest provider of development assistance, spending €6 billion a year in aid to some 150 countries. The EU has a special relationship with the ACP (African, Caribbean and Pacific) countries, a bloc of 650 million people in 78 former colonies, which include 40 of the world's poorest nations. Since the year 2000, the EU has provided ACP countries with preferential trading conditions on products such as sugar, bananas and coffee. But the WTO has ruled that, in the interests of free trade, this arrangement must cease by 2010. Because the ACP countries would lose some US$13 billion as a result, the EU is looking at a package of development aid to compensate.

Financial scandals

The EU handles vast sums of money every year. How this is spent is monitored by the European Court of Auditors, based in Luxembourg. For more than a decade, the Court of Auditors has found so many faults in EU finance that it has often refused to 'sign off' (approve) the accounts. This state of affairs would not be permitted in any large company.

In 1999, all 20 European commissioners and the commission president, Jacques Santer, of Luxembourg, were forced to resign over corruption charges; reforms were promised by the Commission that replaced it, but few have been undertaken. MEPs have also been accused of fiddling their expenses – falsely claiming allowances and travel expenses. In 2003, for example, about €1 million were found to have been misdirected into secret bank accounts by Eurostat, the agency responsible for statistics.

There is always a risk of fraud and malpractice in an organisation as large as the EU. But the scale of these accounting scandals – and no one knows their full extent – has done serious damage to the reputation of the EU and provided further examples of the EU's inefficiency and lack of self-regulation.

Are national currencies more sensitive to national conditions?

When a country has its own currency, it has some control over important financial matters, such as the value of the currency against other currencies (the rate of exchange), and the rates of interest paid on loans. If a country has a strong and valuable currency, it will be able to buy more goods from abroad, but its own goods will also be more expensive to buyers abroad, making exports more difficult. If the country has economic difficulties, it helps to have low rates of interest, so that industries can borrow money cheaply to invest in new projects. Exchange rates and rates of interest, therefore, can be adjusted to suit national circumstances.

With the Euro, there is one rate of exchange and one rate of interest, set by the European Central Bank. Yet it serves as a currency for widely varying economies, from Luxembourg (GDP per capita $48,900) to Greece (GDP per capita $19,100). The fear has always been that the Euro cannot be flexible enough to suit local conditions. Supporters of the Euro will argue that there is great regional variation in economies within any currency – parts of Britain, for instance, are very wealthy, while others are relatively poor, but the pound sterling serves them all. They also point out that on balance, it is better to have a strong currency than a weak one.

Building Bridges

On 1 May 2004, 'E-Day', the German chancellor Gerhard Schroeder and fellow leaders from the Czech Republic and Poland celebrated the enlargement of the EU by crossing three flag-bedecked bridges over the River Neisse, linking all three countries at Zittau, in Germany. It was a symbolic gesture of the kind of constructive friendship and co-operation that the EU can offer. For the EU builds bridges, promoting exchanges not just in trade and politics, but also in culture – in education, music, theatre, art, crafts, ideas, sport, food and drink.

International flags displayed on Bahnhofstrasse in Hannover, Germany. From 1 May 2004, Germany was part of the new, enlarged European Union of 25 member states, which has now increased to 27.

IMMIGRATION: FEARS AND REALITIES

The EU was founded on the principle of the freedom of movement: of goods, services and capital. Following the arrival of the Single Market in 1993, EU citizens are, in principle, free to travel, live and work anywhere they choose in the EU. However, the accession of ten new member states in 2004 gave rise to worries across western Europe that thousands of poor workers would come flooding from eastern Europe as soon as they could.

In the UK, 13,000 eastern European immigrants a year were expected to arrive, but the figure has been more like 600,000 a year to date. In 2004, fears about the state of the British welfare system (in housing, healthcare and unemployment benefit) led the British government to close the door on 'benefit tourism' by stopping migrants from former-communist countries receiving any such benefit before they had worked legally in Britain for at least 12 months. Other 'old' EU countries have introduced similar regulations, and the situation is likely to be reviewed regularly.

Police checking immigration documents on an Austrian-Hungarian border. Following Hungary's accession to the EU in 2004, many of the border controls between Hungary and its EU neighbours have been lifted.

34 TO STAY OR TO GO?

Although many (particularly young) eastern Europeans have taken advantage of the Single Market to live and work in more prosperous parts of the EU, research carried out for the European Commission found that some eastern Europeans were not particularly keen to leave their homes and families. Crime rates in western Europe were a worry and many eastern Europeans feared that life in another country would be too expensive. Sometimes, cross-border traffic is just temporary – many commuters and shoppers travel on a daily basis to destinations in neighbouring countries, but prefer to return home the same day.

When Spain and Portugal joined the EC in 1986, there was widespread fear in the wealthier ten existing member countries that they would be flooded with immigrants. But this did not happen for two reasons: first, people generally prefer to stay among their own communities if they can; and second, both Spain and Portugal enjoyed rapid economic progress, so there were new and better opportunities to make a good living at home. In fact, within 15 years, more immigrants were going to Spain and Portugal than were leaving these countries, causing worries of a completely different kind. The case for eastern Europeans is slightly different, however. After years of communist oppression, the opportunties offered by the wealthier nations of the EU are often difficult to resist – and as the EU looks to expand further, migration is likely to be a worry for some years.

The prosperity of some of the eastern European countries is already causing the accession countries immigration anxieties of their own. The Czech Republic and Hungary are under pressure from foreign workers trying to live there – coming from the Ukraine, Vietnam and other non-EU countries, to do the low-paid, menial jobs that Czechs and Hungarians no longer want to do.

In fact the EU needs migration. The population is ageing and declining, because the people of the EU are not producing enough children. This applies to the new accession countries as well as to the 15 old EU members. The Czech Republic has one of the lowest birthrates in Europe: if it did not allow immigration, the population would decline from 10.25 million in 2003 to 8.1 million in 2050.

Schengen Agreement

Schengen is a place in Luxembourg, and it was here that, in 1985, representatives from Belgium, France, the Netherlands, Germany and Luxembourg met to sign an agreement to abolish border controls – such as passport and customs checks – between their countries. The Schengen Convention of 1990 set up various other kinds of controls within these countries to replace border checks (such as cross-border police co-operation). This did not become effective until 1995, by which time Spain and Portugal had joined the scheme. Since then, a further six countries have joined, plus Norway and Iceland, which are not members of the EU. Britain and Ireland, however, did not sign the agreement: they wanted to maintain border controls as a defence against terrorism and illegal immigration. Switzerland (non-EU) is due to join in 2007 and many of the new EU states are keen.

The terrorist threat

On 11 March 2004, ten bombs exploded on four trains in Madrid, killing 191 people. Blamed on Islamic militants, it was one of the worst terrorist outrages ever perpetrated in Europe. And in 2005, further bombings took place on the London transport network. During this time the US and its allies were conducting a 'War on Terror' following the US terrorist attacks of 11 September 2001 (right). Every decade of the EU's history has been scarred by terrorism, but the 'global terrorism' of groups such as al-Qaeda suggests that the threat today is greater – and destruction could be on a larger scale than ever before.

Terrorism is an international problem, and has to be tackled by international solutions. With its structure of co-operation, the countries of the EU are in a good position to share the information that their police and intelligence services collect on terrorist groups and suspects, and to monitor their movements. The Madrid and London bombings have underlined the need to develop such forms of cross-border co-operation. These issues will now be addressed by the new EU post of Anti-Terrorist Co-ordinator (or 'Czar').

The rise of the far right

One of the main inspirations for the founding of the European Union was the horror and devastation of the Second World War, and the desire never to see such conflict in Europe again. The war was precipitated by the Nazis in Germany, supported by other extreme right-wing groups across Europe, such as the Fascists in Italy. Extreme right-wing groups are often founded on a fervent sense of nationalism, which also entails a fear of foreign influence and a hatred of ethnic and religious minorities within a country. The EU – with its sense of tolerance and international co-operation, its fluid borders and its trend towards centralised government – appears to many modern right-wing groups to represent everything that they oppose. In recent decades a number of right-wing, ultra-nationalist parties have emerged in Europe, such as the National Front in France. They often win support because they voice the opinions of voters that mainstream parties are reluctant to acknowledge. They tend to gain strength in times of economic difficulty, but rarely win more than 15 or 20 per cent of the vote.

TRANSPORT AND TOURISM

Transport is a key factor in the movement of goods and people. This was one of the first areas of development tackled by the EU in the accession countries of eastern Europe, where a new international road and rail network is under construction – using EU structural funds – to transport goods across the region. Telecommunications, airport facilities and the supply of power and fuel are similarly addressed by the EU as trans-border issues.

Tourism is a major industry in the EU, and will play an important role in the development of the accession countries. They have much to offer – historic capital cities, castles, spa towns, mountain scenery (in Slovakia and Slovenia) and excellent beaches (on the Baltic coast). They also have the appeal of the fact that these countries have not been open to foreign visitors for long – and now

Hannover's Hauptbahnhof (main railway station), Germany. Like many cities in the EU, Hannover has developed its transport networks and it now has excellent air, motorway and high-speed rail connections to Europe and the wider world.

tourists from the rest of the EU will find it cheaper and easier to visit them. These visitors will bring with them large sums of money to spend in hotels, restaurants, cafés, concert halls and shops. Cyprus and Malta, which already have highly developed tourist industries, are likely to see this sector grow even more.

While internal borders soften, the EU's external borders have to be strengthened, to control the traffic in illegal immigration, arms and drugs. Illegal immigrants will try to exploit any weakness in the borders to get into the EU. As one of the measures to control external borders, €14 million was spent on a new border post at Narva, between Estonia and Russia and on a new motorway linking Tallinn and St Petersburg.

Illegal immigration is a troubling issue, but it is also a measure of the success of the EU that so many people will risk everything to join it.

European Capitals of Culture

Each year, a city in the EU is appointed European Capital of Culture, and given the opportunity to showcase its unique cultural value to the world. In some years, two or more cities are selected. In 2007, for instance, both Luxembourg and Sibiu (in Romania) have been chosen. In 2008, it will be Liverpool (in the UK) and in 2009, Vilnius (in Lithuania). Each country is allocated with a year, and cities within that country then put in a bid to be selected. Until 2004, cities were selected by the country in question; since 2005, they have been chosen by the Council of Ministers, based on a recommendation of the European Commission, assisted by an independent jury of experts on culture.

Once appointed, a European Capital of Culture will begin feverish activity to present itself to the world in the best light. Assisted by EU funding, it will renovate and restore historic buildings, create a programme of activities (including exhibitions, concerts and theatrical events), commission new monuments and buildings (such as concert halls), and prepare itself for thousands of visitors. Being a European Capital of Culture can transform a city, giving it a new sense of worth and self-confidence.

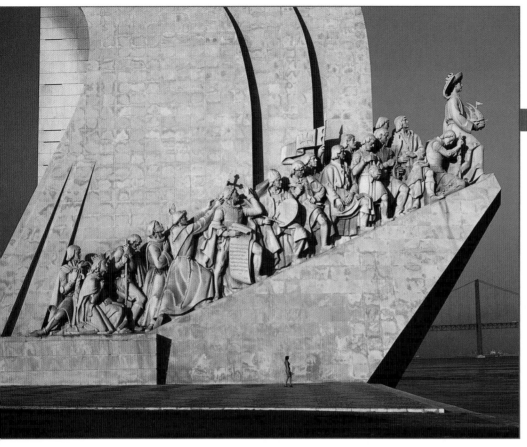

The imposing 'Monument to the Discoveries', Lisbon, Portugal. The monument is situated in the district of Belem, the point from which maritime explorers set forth in their sailing ships, in the 14th and 15th century, to discover the world. The sculpture was built to commemorate the Portuguese Age of Discovery. Now, 600 years later, travel and tourism have become a major industry in the EU.

The Roma

The Czech Republic, Hungary, Slovakia and Poland have been home to a large population of gypsies for hundreds of years; there are 300,000 in the Czech Republic alone. They are known as the Roma, and have their own language and distinct culture. They have also experienced a long history of widespread oppression, are treated with suspicion, and – in some areas – as virtual outcasts. As a result, Roma children are sometimes prevented from getting a proper education, adults find it hard to get work, and many of the Roma live in dire poverty.

When these countries joined the EU, there was concern that the Roma would want to leave their homelands to escape their oppression, and might even be encouraged to do so by their oppressors. However, the Roma, like everyone else, are reluctant to leave their own communities. Migration to other parts of the EU also requires money, education and work skills; the Roma generally have been deprived of all of these.

Culture, identity and the regions

In the past, Europe was like a jigsaw, with each piece representing a separate nation. The edges of the pieces were clearly defined by national borders. Within many of the nations there were also clearly identifiable groups – some almost like

mini-nations with their own language, borders and local government. Spain, for instance, has Catalonia and the Basque country; Belgium has Flanders and Wallonia; France has Brittany and Corsica; the UK has Wales, Scotland and Northern Ireland. In the past, these minority groups were often in dispute with the national government. Such disputes led to campaigns of terrorism in Northern Ireland, the Basque country and Corsica.

The EU has to some degree helped to soothe these disputes. As the EU has become more unified, and national borders have softened, so too have traditional patterns of national identity, helped in many cases by the creation of regional governments. Flanders, for instance, can feel itself as much a part of Europe as a part of Belgium,

and so does not feel it has to define itself so directly in terms of its rivalry with Wallonia. The EU can also intervene directly. Latvia, for example, has a large

Russian minority (amounting to 30 per cent of the population) which voted against joining the EU; but the EU has insisted that they are properly treated, as a condition of Latvia joining the EU. Some people argue that in the EU, the nation states of the past are being replaced by regions, especially in view of the trend to create regional parliaments, as in Scotland and Wales and the German Länder. Many of these regions are, after all, larger than some of the member states of the EU. Some 170 regions now have offices in Brussels. Religion poses a

challenge of a different kind. The EU is predominantly Christian, and yet contains a sizeable minority of Muslims. If the EU can ensure that Muslims are fully engaged in the European project, this may help to address some of the grievances that some Muslims have with their national governments.

39

THE FUTURE

What lies ahead? In the immediate future, the EU must take stock of its revised position. All member states need time to consider how enlargement has changed their own perspective, and their relationship with the EU. Will European farmers lose their livelihoods? Will there continue to be a flood of migration and a 'brain drain' from the accession countries? Will non-ratification of the constitution lead to a complete rethink of the EU?

A peasant farmer and his son drive home a cart loaded with hay, near the city of Zarnesti, north of Bucharest. Romania, which joined the EU in 2007, has an economy largely based on inefficient agriculture.

MAINTAINING MOMENTUM

In 2004, Romano Prodi, former president of the European Commission, recognised that the revised EU needed new goals to avoid stagnation. He declared his vision of the future: a full political union, with a Europe-wide tax and welfare system and cross-border political parties, and a hugely increased budget funded by a tax on companies. These are some of the many issues that the EU is considering as it moves forward in the coming years.

Another way forward is further enlargement to maintain the EU's momentum. Bulgaria and Romania became EU members in 2007. As poor nations (with GDP per head about a third of the EU average), Bulgaria and Romania will put a strain on EU finances. Croatia, Macedonia and Turkey are all trying to have their EU applications accepted, and other western Balkan states, such as Serbia, Bosnia, Montenegro and Albania, are queuing up to join. The appeal of membership is so great that these countries are anxious to show themselves in their best light.

BEYOND EUROPE?

If enlargement continues, it is conceivable that in the future the EU may stretch as far east as the Ural Mountains in Russia. Perhaps one day, the EU may include countries like Georgia, Armenia, Azerbaijan, the Ukraine, Belarus and Moldova. It is possible, too, that the EU might expand to include countries from other continents. Europe is, after all, just a convenient label. Morocco applied to join the EU in 1987, but was rejected out of hand because it was not geographically a part of Europe. But Cyprus is geographically closer to Asia than to Europe, and if Turkey (most of which is in Asia) joins, perhaps Morocco and other North African states might apply. The EU might eventually resemble the shape of the Roman Empire.

It is hard, however, to conceive quite how such a huge Union could be governed. The EU has yet to prove that it can operate successfully with 27 members, let alone 50. At the present time, member states are unable to agree fully on a constitution designed to show how the group of nations should work together. The Roman Empire worked because it had a strong central government, and a powerful army to carry out its orders. At present, there is little call for such a structure in the EU.

The Turkish question

Turkey lies within both Europe and Asia: straddling the Bosphorus (the entrance to the Black Sea) that divides Europe from Asia. Turkey feels that it has strong bonds with Europe and many Turks currently work in the EU (notably in Germany).

Turkey first applied to join the EU in 1987. At first its application was turned down on the basis that it needed to improve its standard of democracy, its human rights record (in particular its treatment of its Kurdish minority) and its economy. The country has made notable improvements on all these fronts. However, although negotiations for Turkey's entry have begun, the success of its application remains in doubt.

For Greece, Turkey is the historic enemy. Turkey is a huge country, with a growing population of 72 million, which would make it one of the largest countries in the Union. In the east, Turkey borders the troubled regions of Syria, Iraq and Iran, and some feel that Turkey may bring those troubles into the arena of European politics.

The main objection, however, is that Turkey is a Muslim country – although this is never expressed as an official reason. Many EU members are simply not certain that the Union – which is essentially a Christian club – can accommodate a nation of around 70 million Muslims. Others welcome a Muslim influence in the EU. Turkey feels some resentment over its continued rejection by the EU, and there are fears that, if rejected again, it may realign itself more closely with the Muslim world of Asia, to Europe's cost.

41

COMPETING ON THE WORLD STAGE

Meanwhile, other major world powers will be watching carefully. The US will want to ensure that the EU remains a friendly power bloc. The emerging Asian economies of China and India want to prosper, and to lift their people out of poverty towards a standard of life comparable to that of Europe. They will be interested in trade and technological exchanges with the EU, but will also be competing for resources and raw materials. Russia, filling the vast tract of land between China and Europe, may wish to align with Europe, or may develop as a major power in its own right. As – and if – the EU grows in strength, it will have to address critical issues of foreign policy, and learn to speak with one voice.

But the EU may not have these kinds of ambitions. It is possible that, with 27 members, the EU will reach its full capacity. It is always hard to know when any enterprise has reached its ideal – or optimum – size. Usually, an enterprise will go one stage too far before it becomes clear that it has exceeded its optimum size. Then it may be too late to go back. Perhaps the EU has reached its optimum size already? Perhaps it has already overreached itself? The story will be told in the very interesting years that lie ahead.

China now has the world's largest economy and is the world's third-largest trading power. What happens in China is of great interest to the rest of the world.

India is emerging as one of the fastest growing economies in the world, thanks to a series of ambitious economic reforms in recent years. Skilled manpower, and a middle-class whose size exceeds the population of the US or the EU, provide India with a distinct advantage in global competition.

What would happen to a country if it left the EU?

No EU member has ever left the Union, but this could certainly happen. For example, many people think that if Britain refuses to accept the constitution, the UK might leave the EU altogether. In terms of the legal, political and economic links of EU membership, leaving the group would be complex, but not impossible. A departing country could even keep the Euro which is tied to the independently-run European Central Bank.

A former EU-member would be able to reclaim its sovereignty over all national matters. But it would lose the financial advantages of membership, such as the Single Market, subsidies and structural funds. It would have to negotiate its own trade agreements with the EU and the rest of the world, and it might well lose foreign investment in factories.

Switzerland and Norway don't appear to have suffered greatly from staying out of the EU, but this might be because both are prosperous and have small populations. What is certain is that old arguments will continue to run: Shall we stay or shall we go? A country might leave the EU and prosper, or it might fade and watch from the sidelines as the EU grows, expands and prospers without it.

CHRONOLOGY

1945 – In Europe, the Second World War ended in May with the surrender of Germany. Much of Europe had been devastated. East Germany, Poland, Hungary and Czechoslovakia came under Soviet control.

1946 – The Cold War began as the Soviet Bloc closed itself off behind the 'Iron Curtain', the frontier that divided Europe into east and west.

1947 – The European Recovery Plan, providing massive American economic aid to western Europe, was announced by US Secretary of State George Marshall. It became known as the Marshall Plan.

1949 – The Council of Europe was founded to promote democracy, human rights and culture in Europe. The North Atlantic Treaty Organisation (NATO) was also founded.

1950 – The French foreign minister Robert Schuman set out his plan to pool French and German coal and steel production, as a way of establishing stability, peace and prosperity.

1951 – France, Germany, Italy, the Netherlands, Belgium and Luxembourg all adopted the Schuman Plan by signing the Treaty of Paris, and formed the European Coal and Steel Community (ECSC). The Common Assembly was established (a forerunner of the European Parliament), along with the Council of Ministers.

1952 – The ECSC began work, with Jean Monnet as its first president.

1957 – The six members of the ECSC signed the Treaty of Rome to establish essential ground-rules of a 'common market', and the European Economic Community (EEC) was formed. The European Atomic Energy Community (EURATOM) was also created, to share the development of nuclear energy among 'The Six'.

1958 – The EEC set up the European Court of Justice to interpret the Treaty of Rome. Along with the Commission, the Council of Ministers and the European Parliament, it now possessed the four main institutions of the future European Union.

1960 – Countries around the EEC formed the European Free Trade Association (EFTA) as a parallel trading bloc, but under a looser form of association.

1961 – The UK made its first application to join the EEC, along with Denmark and Ireland.

1963 – The French president, Charles de Gaulle, blocked the British application to the EEC, largely because he thought that Britain was too independently minded and too closely tied to the US.

1967 – The ECSC, EEC and EURATOM combined to form the European Community (EC). De Gaulle blocked Britain's application for a second time.

1970 – Charles de Gaulle's death ended French opposition to British accession.

1972 – The UK, Denmark, Ireland and Norway signed an accession treaty to join the EC. Norway rejected the idea in a referendum, Denmark and Ireland approved.

CHRONOLOGY

1973 – The UK, Denmark and Ireland joined the EC.

1979 – The European Monetary System (EMS) made the first steps towards the single currency by introducing a European accounting unit called the Ecu, and the Exchange Rate Mechanism (ERM) to fix the value of currencies in relation to each other. The UK was the only member state to stay out of the ERM.

1981 – Greece became the tenth member of the EC.

1985 – Jacques Delors became president of the European Commission, beginning a decade of determined campaigning for a more unified and centralised Europe.

1986 – The accession of Portugal and Spain brought the total number of EC members to twelve. The twelve-star flag was launched. The Single European Act laid out the path towards a single market and a European Union.

1989 – The Berlin Wall was demolished in November, setting in motion the collapse of Communist regimes throughout eastern Europe.

1990 – The Soviet Union was disbanded and replaced by the Commonwealth of Independent States. East and West Germany were reunited. The UK joined the ERM.

1991 – The 12 EC members signed the Maastricht Treaty in December. The EC was to become the European Union (EU), and a timetable was set for the creation of a monetary union with a single currency.

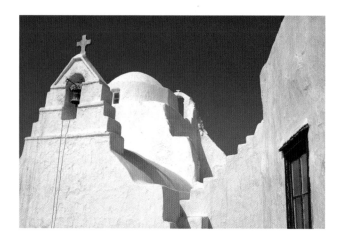

1992 – Suffering from turbulent currency markets in a recession, the UK was forced to abandon the ERM.

1993 – The Maastricht Treaty was ratified after the Danes approved it on a second referendum. The European Council agreed to consider EU membership for new countries, including those of the former Soviet Bloc.

1994 – In a second referendum, Norway rejected a proposal to join the EU.

1995 – Austria, Finland and Sweden joined the EU, bringing membership to 15. The Schengen Convention came into force, lifting border controls between all countries within the EU, except the UK and Ireland.

1999 – Following allegations of fraud and corruption, the president of the European Commission, Jacques Santer, and all 20 commissioners were forced to resign. Santer was replaced by Romano Prodi (who was succeeded in 2004 by José Manuel Durão Barroso).

2002 – Having been introduced as a parallel currency in 1999, Euro notes and coins were introduced on 1 January 2002, replacing national currencies in the 12 countries that had adopted the Euro. The exceptions were Sweden, Denmark and the UK.

2004 – Ten more countries joined the EU, bringing the total membership to 25. The EU draft constitution was finally agreed in June 2004.

2005 – The people of France and the Netherlands said 'no' to the draft constitution.

2007 – Bulgaria and Romania joined the EU and Slovenia joined the Euro.

ORGANISATIONS AND GLOSSARY

Council of Europe – Founded in 1949 and based in Strasbourg, the Council of Europe promotes democracy, human rights and European culture. It was originally a western European organisation, but during the 1990s it allowed a number of former communist countries to join. It was responsible for establishing the European Convention of Human Rights in 1950. There are now 46 members, including all 27 EU members.

Council of Ministers – Based in Brussels, this is the main decision-making body of the EU. It brings together government ministers from the member states to make decisions on key issues. It is also known as the Council of the European Union.

Customs union – Two or more countries can agree to abolish any mutual trade barriers (such as customs duties or tariffs, quotas and so on). This promotes the flow of free trade between them, and also presents a common set of customs tariffs to other trading nations. The EU Single Market is a very large customs union.

Economic and Monetary Union (EMU) – The idea of having a European single currency was first proposed in 1979, and the process of EMU went through a number of stages. This included the Exchange Rate Mechanism (ERM), which fixed the exchange rates of the various European currencies. This was superseded by the introduction of the 'single currency', the Euro.

European Coal and Steel Community (ECSC) – The founding organisation of the EU was set up by the Treaty of Paris in 1951. It lasted until the creation of the EC in 1967.

European Commission – This is the civil service and main policy-maker of the EU. It is headed by the president of the Commission and 27 commissioners.

European Community (EC) – In 1967 the ECSC, EEC and the European Atomic Energy Community (EURATOM) were combined to form the EC, the predecessor of the EU.

European Council – At least twice a year heads of EU governments and their foreign ministers meet at a summit, called a European Council, to discuss and decide on major issues, and to sign treaties.

European Court of Human Rights – Based in Strasbourg, this is the court of the Council of Europe, and resolves issues concerning the European Convention of Human Rights; it is independent of the EU.

European Court of Justice – Based in Luxembourg, this is the EU's court. It oversees the legal aspects of EU treaties and directives, and rules on any aspect of EU law.

European Economic Area (EEA) – This is the frontier-free zone established by the EU and EFTA in 1994.

European Economic Community (EEC) – The 1957 Treaty of Rome established a trading zone called a 'Common Market', known as the EEC. The term was used for a decade, until the creation of the EC.

European Free Trade Association (EFTA) – EFTA is a trading bloc and customs union that operates in conjunction with the EU. It was founded in 1960, forming an outer circle around 'The Six' (the founder members of the EU). It included Austria, Denmark, Finland, the UK, Portugal and Sweden, which have since left EFTA to join the EU. The current EFTA members are Iceland, Liechtenstein, Norway and Switzerland.

European Union (EU) – When the Maastricht Treaty was ratified in 1993, the EC became the EU, reflecting the drive towards a single market and greater unification.

Free market – Where trade is regulated entirely by supply and demand, and without interference from government, it is said to be a 'free market'.

General Agreement on Tariffs and Trade (GATT) – A series of meetings was held by leading trading countries from 1947 to 1995 in order to try to establish the ground rules for trade throughout the world, and to reduce the trading imbalances caused by tariffs (such as import duties) and other barriers to international free trade (such as quotas and subsidies). The last round of negotiations, the 'Uruguay Round' in 1995, established the World Trade Organisation.

Gross Domestic Product (GDP) – GDP is the value of the total output (good and services) of a nation in a year. It is sometimes divided by the population to give GDP per capita (or GDP per head), which is used to give a figure for measuring the comparative prosperity of a country.

G-8 – The world's leading industrial nations meet regularly as the Group of Eight (G-8). They are: Canada, France, Germany, Italy, Japan, Russia, the UK and the USA. The EU is also treated as a member.

Maastricht – The Maastricht Treaty of 1991 (named after the city in the Netherlands where it was signed) established the European Union, and made the people of the 12 nations 'citizens of the European Union'. It also made major advances towards the Single Market, setting out the preparations for the single currency.

North Atlantic Treaty Organisation (NATO) – NATO was founded in 1949 as a defence organisation that brought together the USA, Canada and their allies in western Europe to face the military threat posed by the Soviet Union. There are 26 member countries; 21 of these are members of the EU. Thus NATO remains central to the EU's defence strategy. Its headquarters are in Brussels.

Protectionism – If a government wishes to protect its own industries from foreign competition, it can introduce a variety of measures (such as customs duties, quotas and other trade barriers) to put foreign produce at a disadvantage. This is called protectionism.

Single Market – To promote trade between its members, the EU is gradually trying to create a single market, free of tariffs and restrictions, with uniform regulations and a single currency throughout.

Subsidiarity – The principle of subsidiarity was formulated during negotiations for the Maastricht Treaty of 1991. It established that decision-making should be made at the appropriate level: local, regional or national.

Treaty of Rome – This is the founding and primary treaty of the EU, signed originally by 'The Six' in 1957. All subsequent treaties (such as the Maastricht Treaty) are in fact amendments to the Treaty of Rome.

Veto – Some decisions by the Council of Ministers can only be accepted if all members agree. This usually applies to important national issues, such as tax, criminal justice and EU funding. If ministers disagree – even just one minister – they can veto the measure, and it will not be passed.

World Trade Organisation (WTO) – The WTO was established in 1995 to continue the work of GATT. Based in Geneva, with 150 members, its task is to monitor national trading policies, to help to settle trading disputes, and to promote the aims of GATT in reducing tariffs and other barriers to trade. It has run into conflict with the EU over its subsidies and trade barriers for agricultural products, notably the CAP and restrictions imposed on GM crops and food.

INDEX

Photo Credits:
Abbreviations: l-left, r-right, b-bottom, t-top, c-centre, m-middle. Front cover main ml, mr and back cover t, 1ml, 2ml, 2-3b, 3tr, 4tr, 8ml, 8tr, 8c both, 8mr. 8bl, 8br, 18t, 19 both, 23r, 25tr, 26tl, 31br, 44tr – European Parliament. Front cover c – Stockbyte. 1c, 6tr, 17tr, 22mt, 29mr, 35mt, 37tr, 37c, 38tl, 39tl, 39tr, 39cr, 39bl, 39br, 41 all, 45 both – Corbis. 1mr, 4bl, 5tr, 6bl, 9t, 24bl, 33ml, 36-37b, 39cl, 43 – Corel. 2bl, 20mr, 22bl – PBD. 7br – National Archive and Records Administration. 8tl, 15ml, 18c, 20tr, 21tr, 24mr, 27tl, 28bl, 28br, 30tr, 35ml, 36tl, 38ml – Photodisc. 10-11, 13br – © European Community, 2004. 14mr, 25mr – epa photo/afi/elmars rudzitis © European Community, 2004. 15tl, 16t – epa photo/attila kisbenedek © European Community, 2004. 15br, 42b – Flat Earth. 20bl – R D Ward/US Navy. 21tl – © Beirne Brendan/CORBIS SYGMA. 27bl – Corbis Royalty Free. 28t – epa photo/ stanislaw ciok © European Community, 2004. 30b – epa photo/lino arrigo azzopardi © European Community, 2004. 31tl – epa photo/ctk/samuel kubani © European Community, 2004. 34t – J. B. Russell/Corbis Sygma. 35br – Andrea Booher/FEMA. 38br – Peter Turnley/CORBIS. 39ml – Photo Essentials. 40tr – epa/afi/normunds mezins © European Community, 2004. 40bl – epa photo/robert ghement © European Community, 2004. 44bl – MSgt Phil Mehringer/USMC.